LEARN HOW TO PLAY THE BLUEGRASS WAY

ASAP

Fiddle Tunes

MADE EASY FOR
BLUEGRASS BANJO

BY EDDIE COLLINS

ISBN 978-1-57424-260-7
SAN 683-8022

Cover by James Creative Group

Photo by Steve Oleson

Table of Contents
& CD Track List

SOME WORDS ABOUT FIDDLE TUNES

If you've been learning banjo for a while, especially if you're out there jamming, you've undoubtedly come across the expression fiddle tune. Why should we have an interest in such tunes, being that we're banjo pickers, not cigar box thrashers? The answer lies in the fact that many of the early instrumental (not vocal) tunes you'll learn on the banjo have evolved from tunes originally composed on the fiddle. The lineage of such tunes can be traced back hundreds of years. The following is an historical perspective on the evolution of fiddle tunes and how to recognize their key features.

The most important characteristic of a tune bearing the fiddle tune moniker is its structure. Most fiddle tunes have two distinctively different sections with each section played twice. While an occasional fiddle tune, such as *Eighth of January* or *Cluck Old Hen* contain four-measure segments, most, such as *Old Joe Clark* and *Blackberry Blossom*, are composed of eight-measure sections. Many are often referred to as reels or hornpipes–two traditional dances in the British Isles. In most bluegrass and old-time jam circles, reels and hornpipes are treated the same in regards to the tempo and underlying rhythmic feel, whereas Irish players will purposely play hornpipes at a slower tempo to allow for more melodic ornamentation.

The two different sections of any given fiddle tune are simply labeled Part A and Part B. If a song, such as *Dill Pickle Rag*, has a third part, it would be labeled Part C. One hint in identifying sections is that there most often will be a different set of background chords for each section. Sometimes the change may be slight, such as there being an F chord in Part B for one measure in *Old Joe Clark*, rather than the D chord found in Part A. There are a few tunes, like *Boil 'Em Cabbage* and *Devil's Dream*, where the chords are the same for each section. Thus, as a rhythm player, you'd be playing the same eight-measure pattern over and over and would have to listen carefully to identify when the total of four parts (two Part A's and two Part B's) has been played.

There is occasional confusion as to which part of the song is Part A and which is Part B. Of all of the recordings I've ever heard of *Soldier's Joy*, about half begin on one of the two distinct melody parts, while the other half begin on the second of the two melodies. At that point, you simply label what you hear first as Part A with the next section being Part B.

Most fiddle tunes were composed without lyrics, others are equally known for their engaging lyrics, like *Turkey In The Straw*. To me, it's obvious that sometimes lyrics were penned long after the melody had become standard fiddle tune fare. Songs in this category include *Whiskey Before Breakfast* and *Red Haired Boy*. *Buffalo Gals* was likely composed with the familiar lyrics and thus each part is only performed once, rather than having the traditional repeat.

Many fiddle tunes are most often performed in the keys of A and D, as these are easy keys for fiddles and mandolins. Since we more easily play out of G, have your capo ready to be placed at the 2nd fret to bring them up to normal pitch. Be sure to practice songs like *Old Joe Clark* and *Bill Cheatham* with the capo at the 2nd fret so it will feel right when performing with others.

All of the tunes are presented in the key of which they are most commonly performed. You will only need to use a capo for the key of A pieces. Tune the 5th string to A during *Whiskey Before Breakfast*, but keep the other four strings in standard G tuning (a DGBD). Happy Picking!

ABOUT THIS BOOK

This book is designed to provide beginning and intermediate level players with solos for the most popular fiddle tunes heard at bluegrass jam sessions. While these songs appear in many other books, they are rarely stripped down to just the essentials needed to play a competent solo and join the jam. To speed the process of learning these tunes, *Basic Version* solos have been modified in the following ways:

- The solos contain lots of quarter notes, so there are fewer notes to learn.
- Most solos begin on beat 1, so there is less worry about in regards to when to come in.
- Only simple, basic rolls are used.

Intermediate Level solos are characterized by the following:

- More 8th notes and continuous, possibly more complex, rolls are used.
- The left hand may be required to hold slightly more difficult formations.

TABLATURE AND TUNING

Tablature is a representation of the strings on the banjo. String number 1 is on top of the series of parallel lines. A number on the line represents the fret that is to be played on the given string. An "S" or "H" represents a Slide or Hammer-on. For more on tablature, see the guide on page 3. Standard G tuning (g DGBD – for strings 5 through 1) is used on all the songs. Any alterations, such as the use of a capo, is noted underneath the song's title.

COUNTING THE BEATS

All the pieces in this book could be played in 4/4, or "Common" time with four beats in each measure. This dictates that you count four beats per measure with a series of 8th notes being counted 1 & 2 &, etc.

PLAYING WITH A BOUNCE

Most bluegrass songs, especially when performed slowly, are played with an uneven feel called a *shuffle* or *bounce*. The music is written using 8th notes, but two 8th notes are played as a triplet with the first two notes tied. Since few 8th notes are used in these arrangements and not at all in the rhythm, the bounce will mainly be a concern of the banjo players. It is best to imitate the feel of the beat by replicating what you hear on the practice CD.

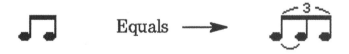

PERFORMANCE NOTES

Performance notes help you interpret each song and alert of potential tricky parts. These songs are primarily performed at jams as instrumentals. As such, no lyrics are provided.

THE PRACTICE CD

The CD allows you to hear each solo at slow and fast speeds. Tune to an electronic tuner and you will be in tune to the CD. The instruments are recorded with separation. Adjust your balance knob for more banjo to learn the piece, or more guitar to practice performing your solos. The track numbers are listed in the Table of Contents and on each individual solo.

TABLATURE GUIDE

Symbol	Name	Explanation
|	Measure Line	Separates notes into an equal number of beats
||	Double Bar	Marks start or end of a section
||:	Begin Repeat	Marks start of part played twice
:||	End Repeat	Marks end of repeated section
1.	1st Ending	Play this ending 1st time through
2.	2nd Ending	Play this ending 2nd time through
$\frac{3}{4}$	Time Signature	Top # = # of beats per measure; Bottom # = the type of note that gets 1 count
♪	Eighth Note	Receives 1/2 count
|	Quarter Note	Receives 1 count
⎵	8ths Beam	Count 2 per beat
⎅	16ths Beam	Count 4 per beat
3	Triplet	Count 3 per beat
⦚	Quarter Rest	Rest 1 beat
⅄	Eighth Rest	Rest 1/2 beat
▬	Half Rest	Rest 2 beats
•	Dot	Add 1/2 value of original note
⌢	Tie	Combines note values of two notes into one note
0	Zero	Play string open
2	Numeral	Number of fret to be played
c	Choke	Left hand bends note as right hand strikes string
s	Slide	Slide left-hand finger to sound second note
h	Hammer-On	Add second note without restriking the string
p	Pull-Off	Pull finger off to sound second note
⁓ b	Brush	Strum strings so as to hear each string

The Left-Hand Fingers
(palm up)

1 2 3 4

The Right-Hand Fingers
(palm up)

M I

T

ARKANSAS TRAVELER

Traditional

Basic Version

Arranged by Eddie Collins

Key of D: Standard G Tuning

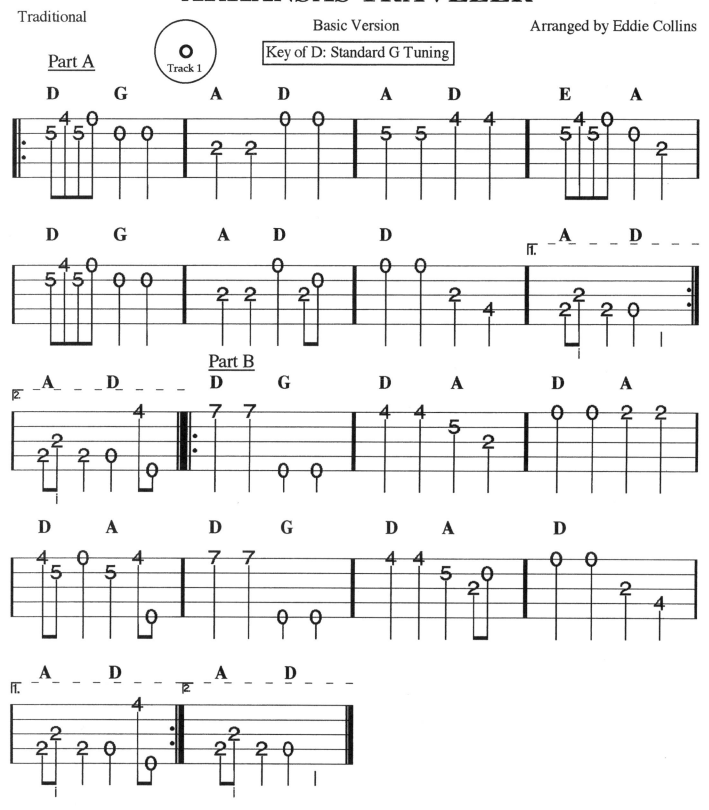

This solo is in the key of D, but without having to retune the banjo or use a capo. Begin by holding your 1st finger on fret 4 of string 1 and your 2nd finger on fret 5 of string 2. The first finger moves to play fret 2 and the 3rd finger plays the 4th fret on string 4. The 4th finger will play the 7th fret in Part B. Form a bar with your 1st finger for the A chord during each ending. Practice playing the chords for rhythm as the frequent changes make it a bit of a challenge.

ARKANSAS TRAVELER

Traditional

Intermediate Level

Arranged by Eddie Collins

Key of D: Standard G Tuning

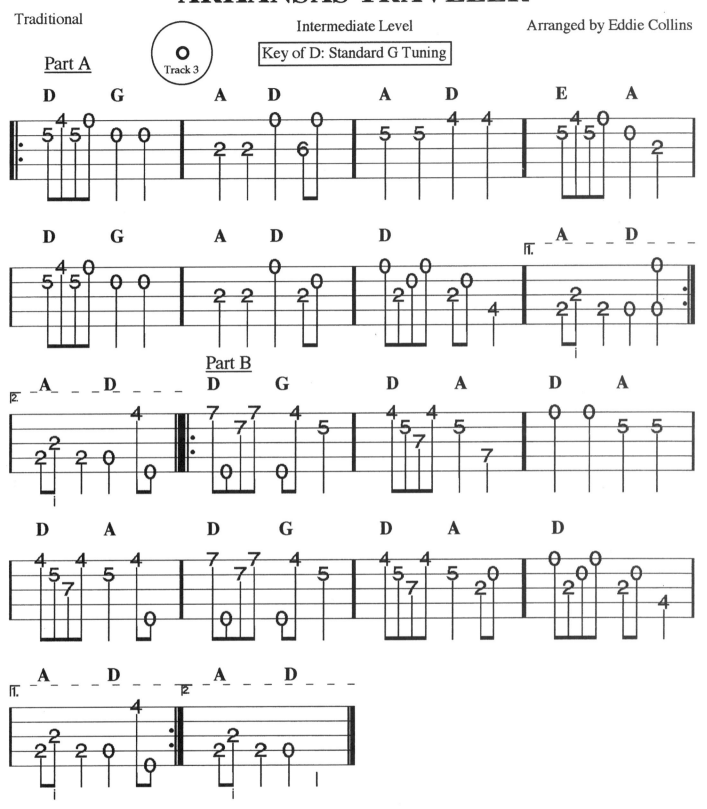

This is in the key of D, but without retuning the banjo or using a capo. Much of the song is performed between frets 4 and 7 using fingers 1 – 4, respectively. Finger 1 moves to play fret 2 and the 3rd finger plays the 4th fret on string 4. The 4th finger bars strings 1 and 2 at the 7th fret to begin Part B. Form a bar with your 1st finger for the A chord during each ending. Practice playing the chords for rhythm as the frequent changes make for a challenge.

BACK UP AND PUSH

Traditional

Basic Version

Arranged by Eddie Collins

Key of C: Standard G Tuning

Part A

Track 5

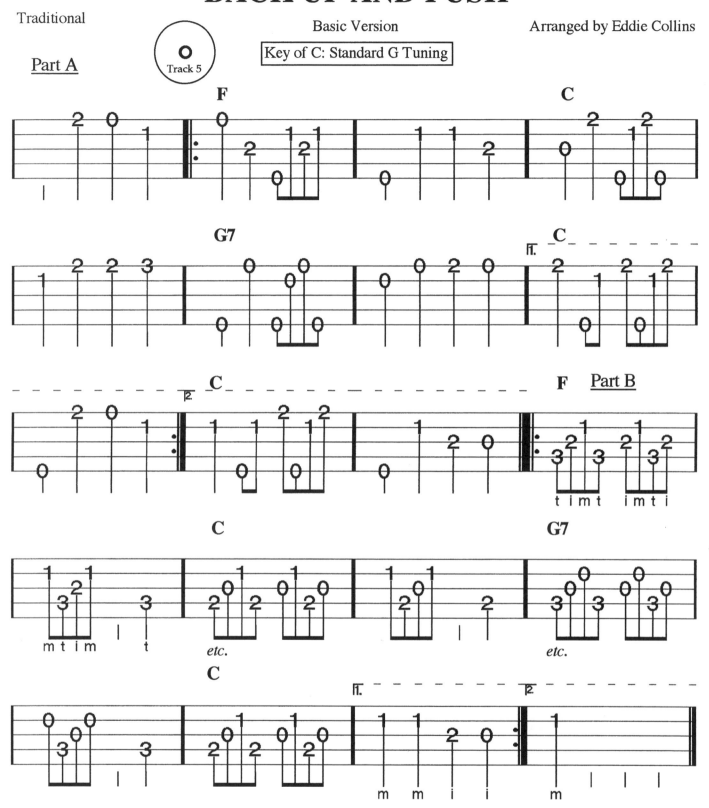

Begin on beat 2. Listen to the recording to understand the Repeats. Only hold fingers 1 and 2 of the initial F chord, whereas you'll need fingers 1, 2, and 3 of the F chord in Part B. The right-hand pattern for each chord in Part B is the equivalent of the theme to the big band song "In The Mood." Keep your Index finger on string 3 and Middle finger on string 2 throughout Part B. There is only one note under the final ending as the next soloist enters on beat 2.

BACK UP AND PUSH

Traditional

Intermediate Level

Arranged by Eddie Collins

Key of C: Standard G Tuning

Part A Track 7

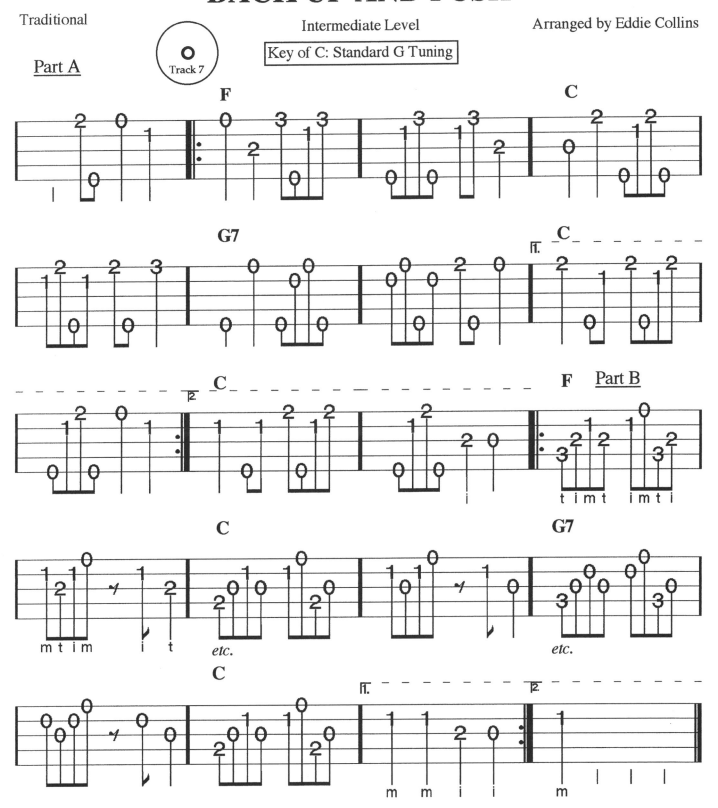

Begin on beat 2. Listen to the recording to understand the Repeats. Hold fingers 1, 2 and 4 of the initial F chord and then fingers 1, 2, and 3 of the F chord in Part B. The right-hand pattern for each chord in Part B follows the "In The Mood" sound, but your right-hand fingers rotate from strings 4, 3, and 2 to strings 3, 2 and 1. Notice the 1st string is left open during the F and C chords. Only one note appears in the final ending as the next soloist enters on beat 2.

BILL CHEATHAM

Traditional

Basic Version

Arranged by Eddie Collins

Key of A: Capo 2nd Fret

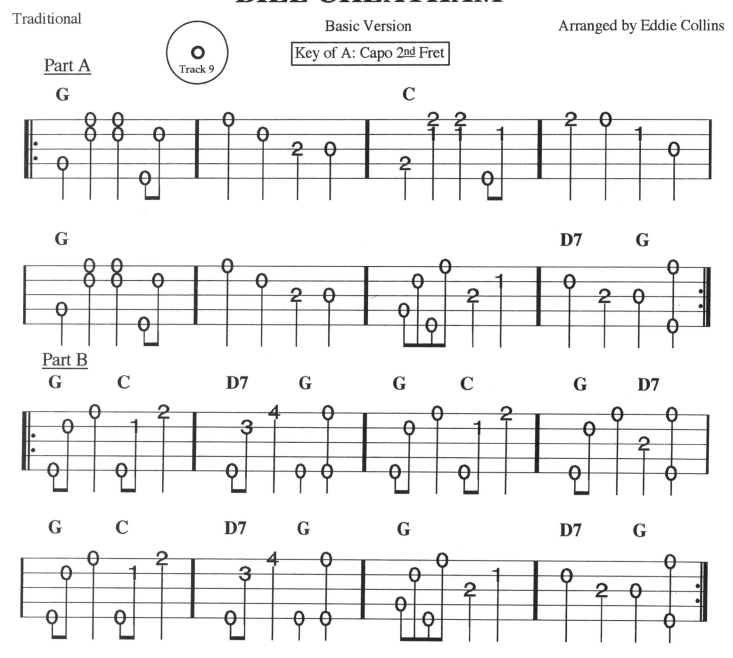

Hold a C chord beginning with beat 3 of the first measure of Part B. Move fingers 1 and 3 up respectively to frets 3 and 4 in the following measure during the D7 chord. Be sure to also practice the rhythm to Part B as the chords change twice per measure.

BILL CHEATHAM

Traditional

Intermediate Level

Arranged by Eddie Collins

Track 11

Key of A: Capo 2nd Fret

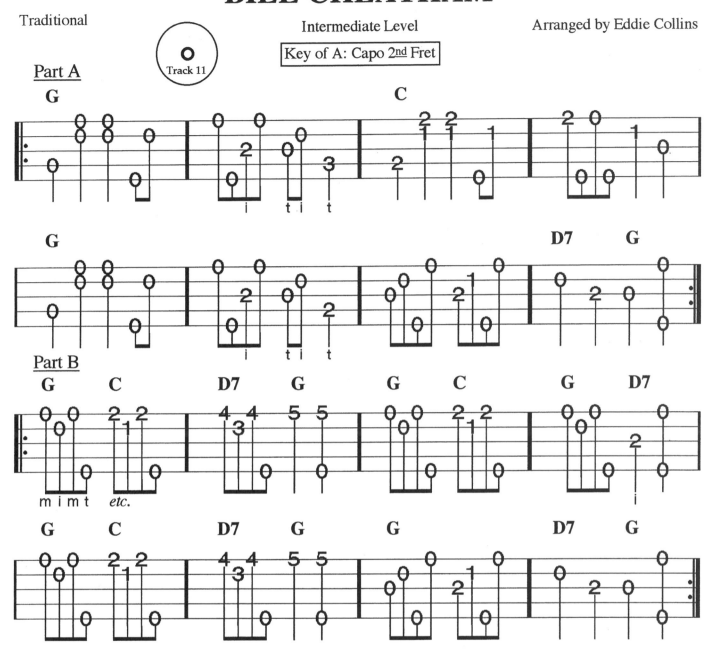

The four-note roll that begins Part B is played MIMT, which is a common roll used by Doug Dillard. The 3rd finger moves from fret 2 during the C chord in Part B up to fret 4 and eventually fret 5. Note how the Index finger of the right hand has to play the 3rd string on several occasions, since the Thumb just played the 5th string on the previous quick note.

13

BLACKBERRY BLOSSOM

Traditional

Basic Version

Arranged by Eddie Collins

Key of G

Part A

Track 13

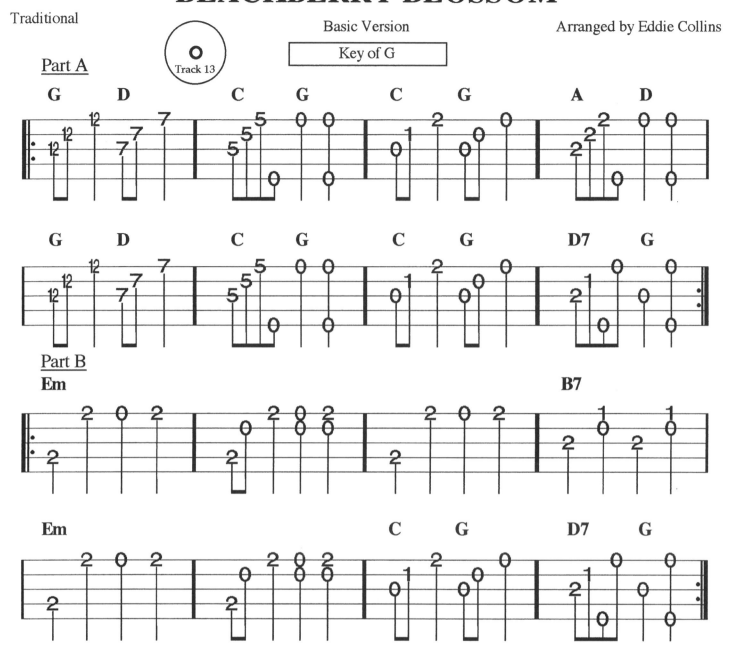

Your 1st finger bars strings 3, 2 and 1 at frets 12, 7 and 5 to begin the song. Notice that the chord changes every two beats during Part A, so you will want to familiarize yourself with rhythm as well as the notes of the solo. Hold an Em chord to begin Part B with your 2nd finger on string 4 and 3rd finger on string 1. You could play a B chord instead of the B7 when playing rhythm.

BLACKBERRY BLOSSOM

Traditional

Intermediate Level

Arranged by Eddie Collins

Track 15

Key of G

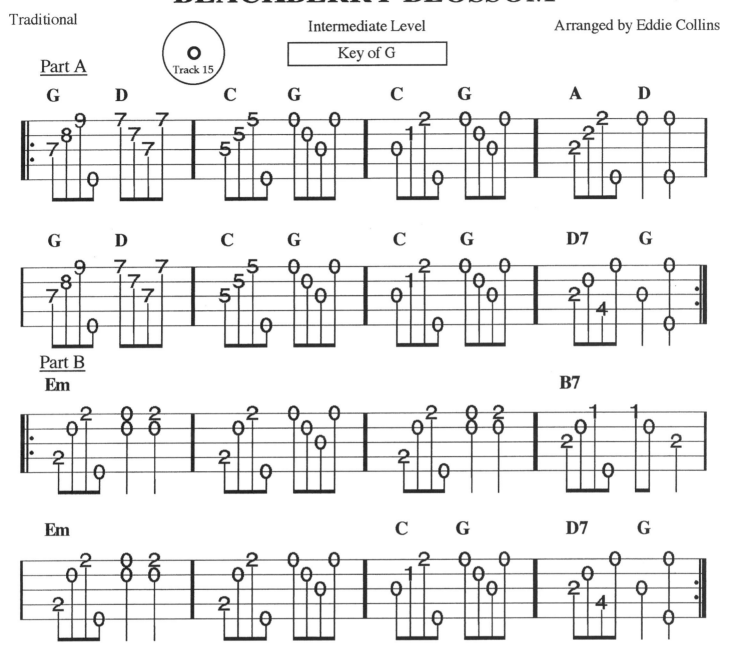

This version utilizes the continuous use of a forward/backward roll in the right hand. The first G chord is played as a "D" shape with fingers 1, 2 and 4 playing frets 7, 8 and 9 respectively. Use finger 1 on fret 2 and finger 3 on fret 4 during the last measure of each section. Add and remove your 3rd finger from the 1st string during the Em chord as needed. The open 5th string clashes with the notes of the B7 chord, but it is only momentary and helps keep the flow of the right-hand roll going.

BUFFALO GALS

Traditional

Basic Version

Arranged by Eddie Collins

Track 17

Key of G

Part A

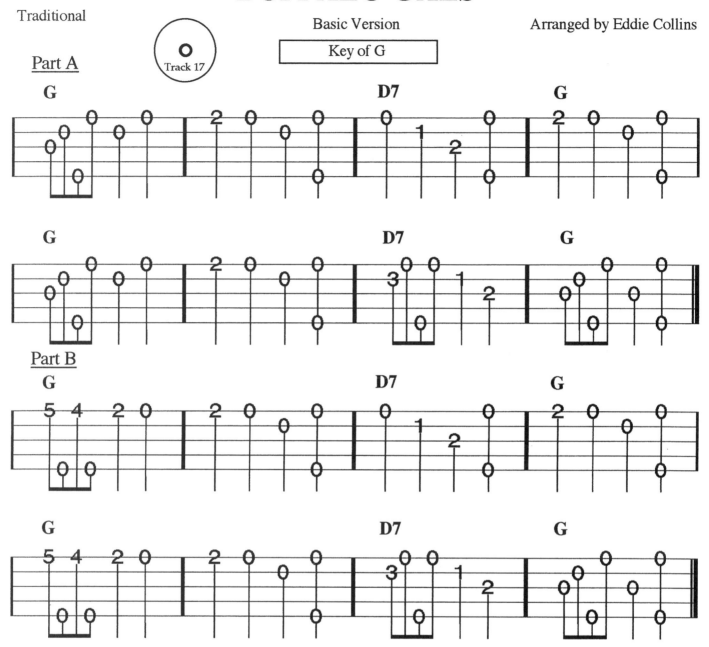

Part B

Most American fiddle tunes can be traced to Appalachia with many having their roots in the British Isles. This one clearly has a theme from the western prairies. Only the first measure of each line in Part B is different than all the other measures in Part A. Use fingers 4, 3 and 1 to play frets 5, 4, and 2 to begin Part B. Notice that the chords are the same for both sections. Neither section repeats. Lyrically, Part A would be the melody to the verse and Part B would be the melody to the chorus.

BUFFALO GALS

Traditional

Intermediate Level

Arranged by Eddie Collins

Key of G

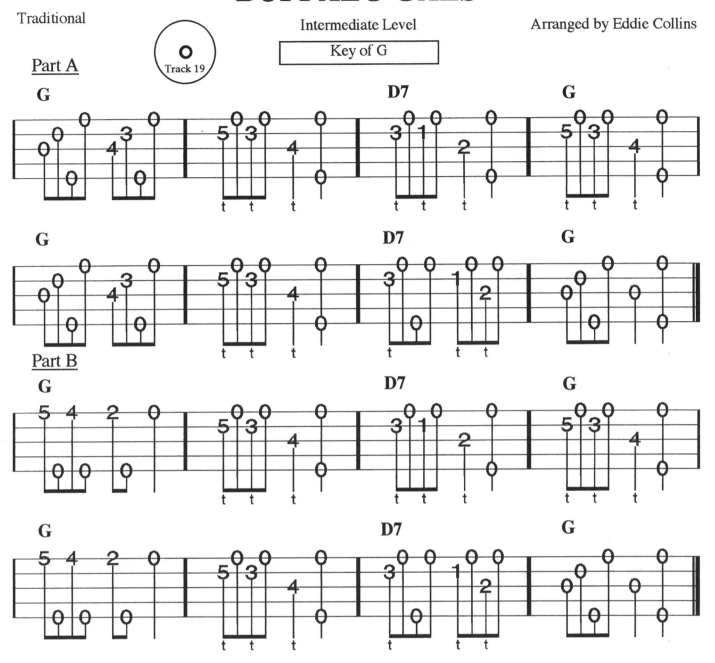

Move fingers 1 and 2 up to frets 3 and 4 during the first measure. Your fingers will look as though they have moved a D7 chord up two frets. Continue to hold frets 3 and 4 as you add your 3rd finger to fret 5 on string 2. Then move the same fingerings down to frets 3, 2 and 1 in the third measure of each line. Playing the Thumb on the many 2nd string notes helps to maintain a solid rhythmic feel. Neither section repeats.

DEVIL'S DREAM

Traditional

Basic Version

Arranged by Eddie Collins

Key of A: Capo 2nd Fret

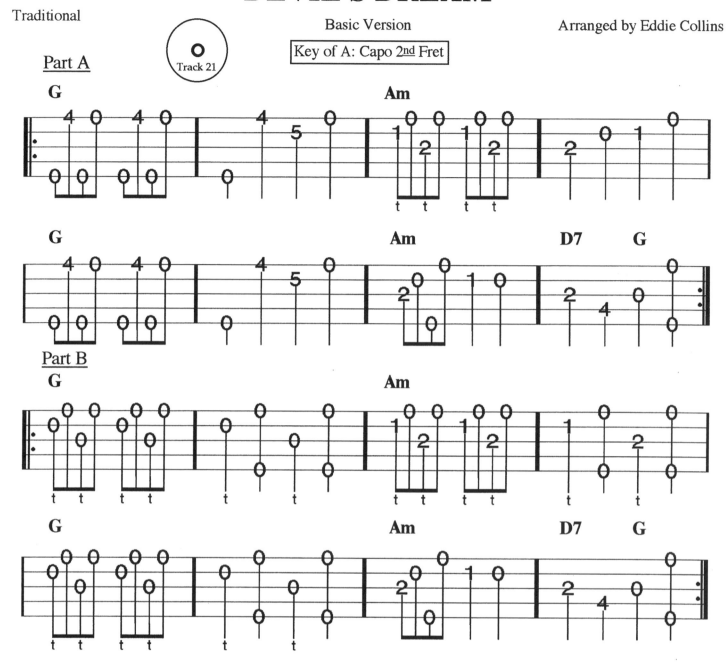

Use your 1st finger on the 4th fret of string 1 and your 2nd finger on the 5th fret of string 2. Your fingers play what looks like a D7 during the Am chord. Playing the Thumb on the many 2nd string notes helps to maintain a solid rhythmic feel.

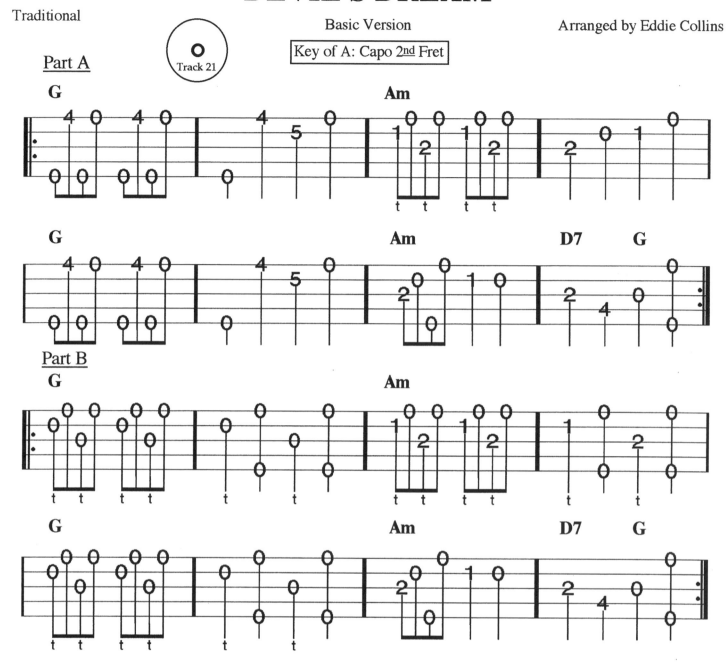

DEVIL'S DREAM

Traditional

Track 23

Intermediate Level

Arranged by Eddie Collins

Key of A: Capo 2nd Fret

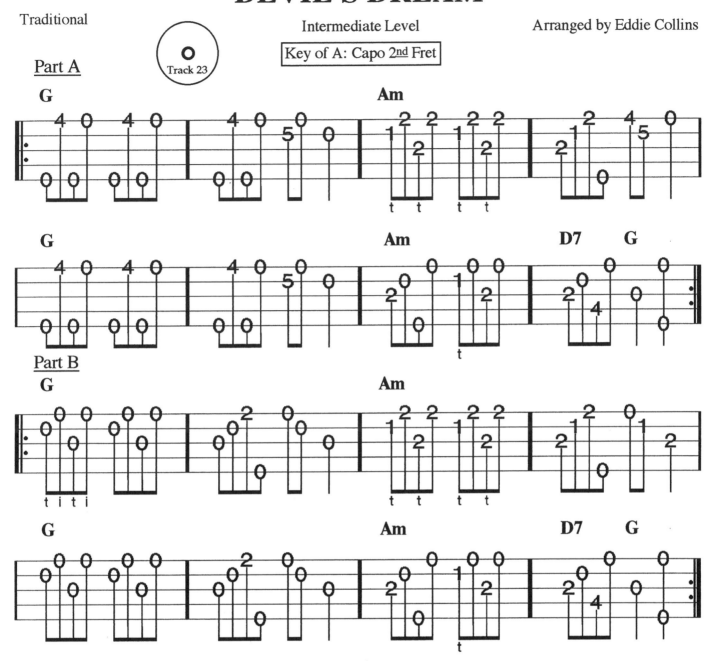

Use your 1st finger on the 4th fret of string 1 and your 2nd finger on the 5th fret of string 2. Play a partial Am chord beginning in the third measure with the 3rd finger added to the 2nd fret of the 1st string to what otherwise would be a D7 chord. Your 4th finger plays the 4th fret in measures 8 and 16.

EIGHTH OF JANUARY

Traditional

Basic Version

Arranged by Eddie Collins

Track 25

Key of D: Standard G Tuning

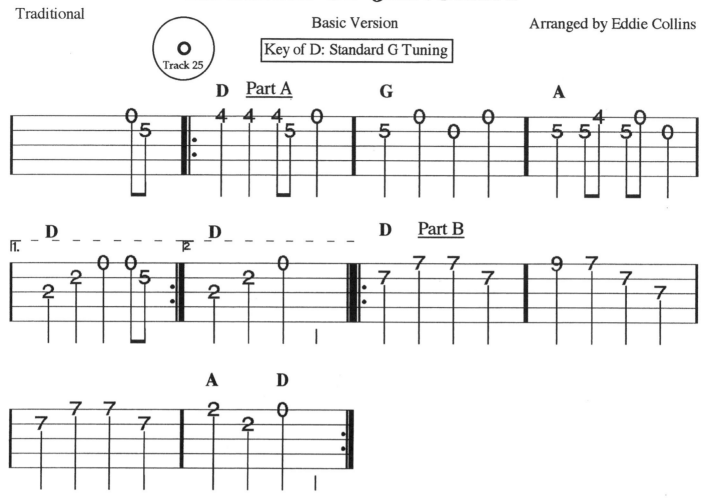

This solo is in the key of D, but without having to retune the banjo or use a capo. Use your 1st finger to play fret 4 and 2nd finger to play fret 5. The 1st finger moves to play the 2nd fret. Begin Part B by holding your 1st finger as a bar at the 7th fret. The 3rd finger then plays fret 9. Each section is only four measures long before repeating.

EIGHTH OF JANUARY

Traditional

Intermediate Level

Arranged by Eddie Collins

Track 27

Key of D: Standard G Tuning

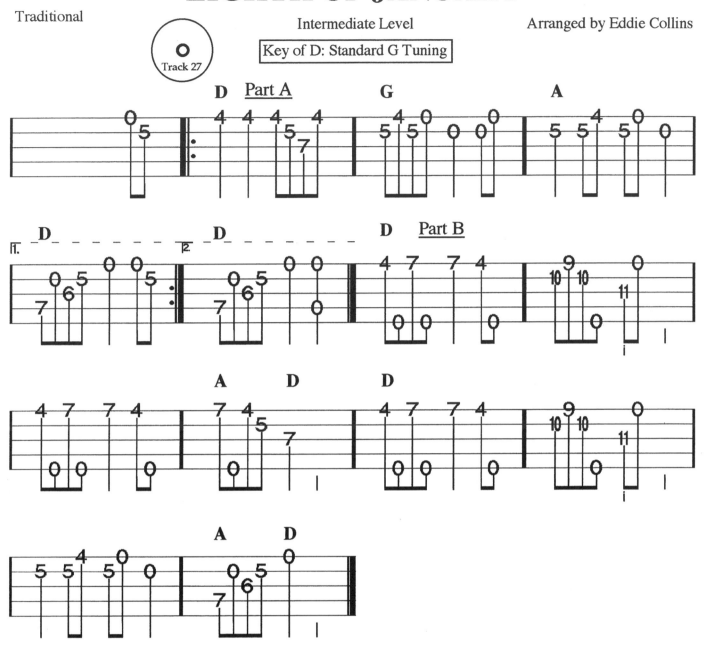

This solo is in the key of D, but without retuning or using a capo. Begin on beat 4. Most of the song is performed between frets 4 and 7 using fingers 1 – 4, respectively. Finger 2 moves up to fret 10 in the second and sixth measures of Part B with finger 1 playing fret 9 and finger 3 playing fret 11. Part B is presented as a series of eight measures, rather than a repeated four-measure section.

21

GOLDEN SLIPPERS

Traditional

Basic Version

Arranged by Eddie Collins

Key of G

Track 29

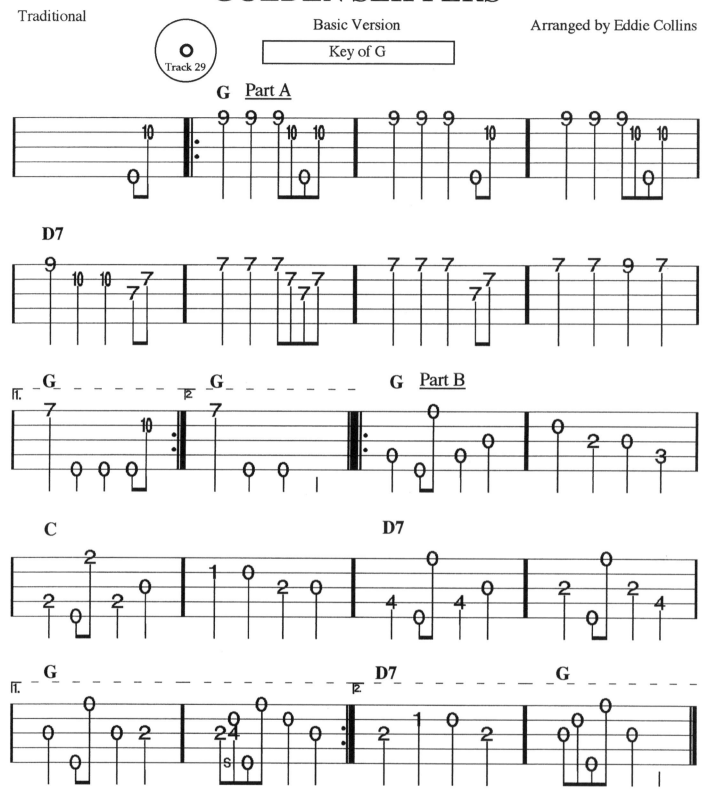

Listen to the recording to understand how to work the Repeats. Begin on beat 4 with your 2nd finger on fret 10 and 1st finger on fret 9. Bar the 7th fret with your 1st finger during the D7. Use the same number finger as fret being played throughout Part B, except use your 3rd finger to play fret 2 on string 1 during the C chord.

GOLDEN SLIPPERS

Traditional

Intermediate Level

Arranged by Eddie Collins

Track 31

Key of G

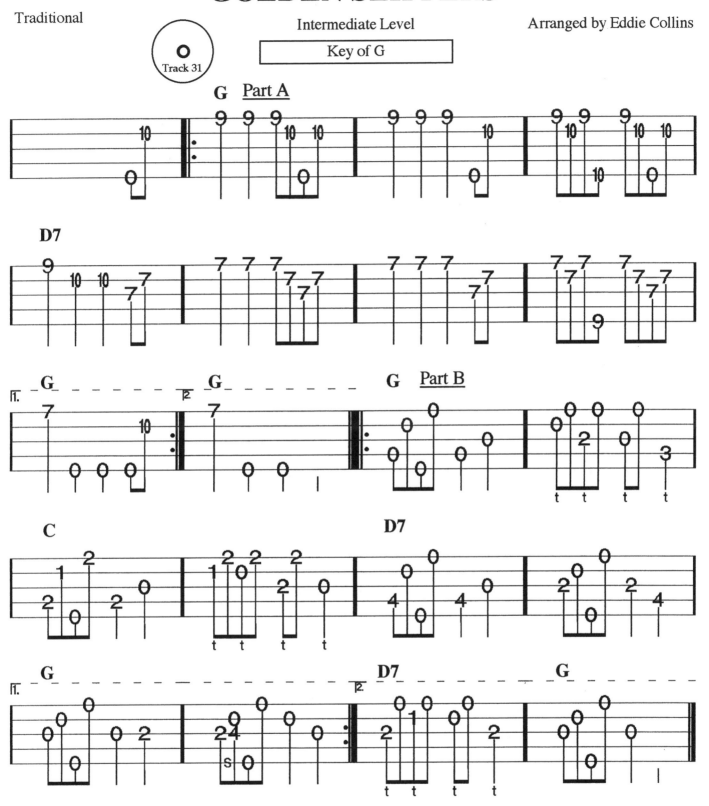

Listen to the recording to understand the Repeats. Begin on beat 4 with finger 2 on fret 10 and finger 1 on fret 9. The left-hand thumb plays fret 10 on string 5. Bar fret 7 with your 1st finger during the D7. The 3rd finger then is added to fret 9 on string 5 and later string 1. Use the same number finger as fret played throughout Part B, except use finger 3 to play fret 2 on string 1 during the C chord. The right-hand Thumb plays numerous 2nd string notes in Part B.

GOOD-BYE LIZA JANE

Traditional

Basic Version

Arranged by Eddie Collins

Key of A: Capo 2nd Fret

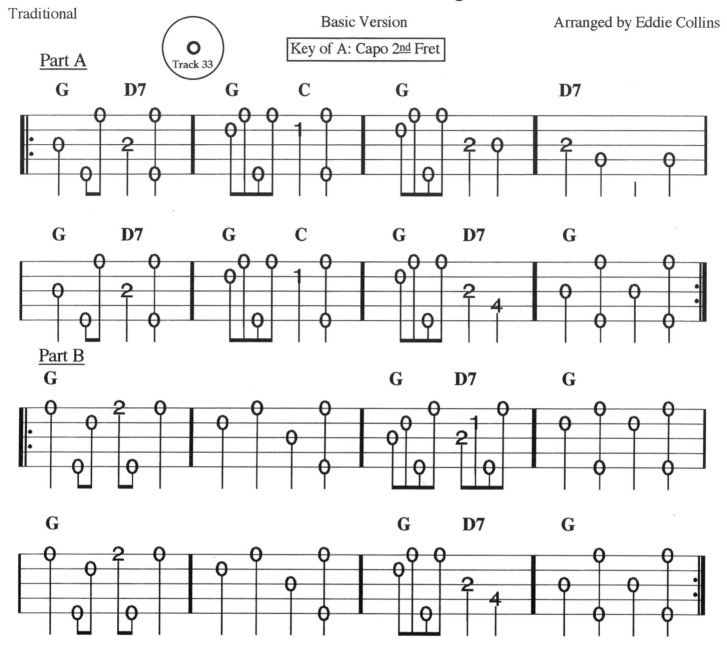

Use the same number finger as fret you are playing throughout this piece. For example, use your pinky on fret 4 in the seventh and fifteenth measures. There is no note on beat 3 of the fourth measure during Part A.

GOOD-BYE LIZA JANE

Traditional

Intermediate Version

Arranged by Eddie Collins

Track 35

Key of A: Capo 2nd Fret

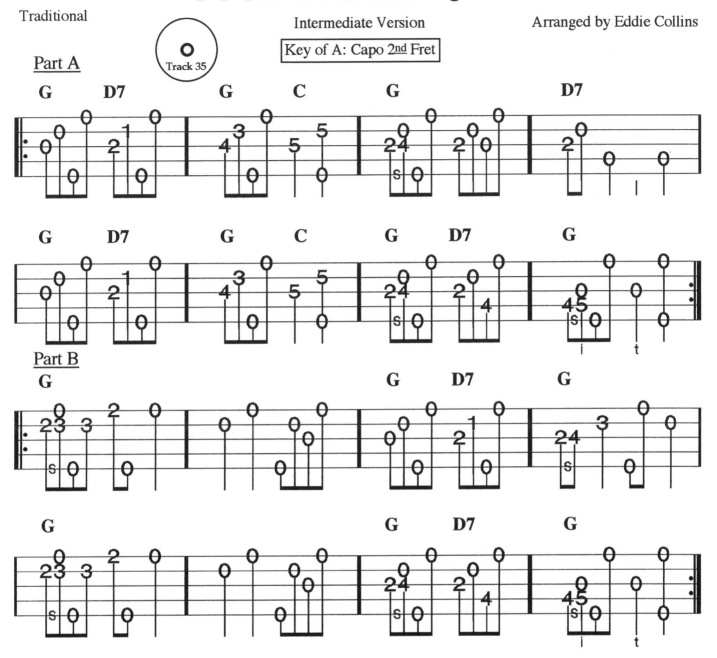

Move fingers 1 and 2 up to frets 3 and 4 during the second measure. Finger 2 then moves up to fret 5 on string 3 as you add your 3rd finger to the 5th fret of string 2. Hold your 2nd finger at fret 3 after completing the slide to begin Part B. Then add your 1st finger to fret 2 on string 1. The right-hand Index finger strikes string 3 right as you complete the 4–5 slide with the left hand during measures 8 and 16.

In this version, finger 1 will play fret 2 and finger 3 will play fret 4 during the seventh and fifteenth measures.

HAMILTON COUNTY BREAKDOWN

Traditional

Track 37

Basic Version

Key of G

Arranged by Eddie Collins

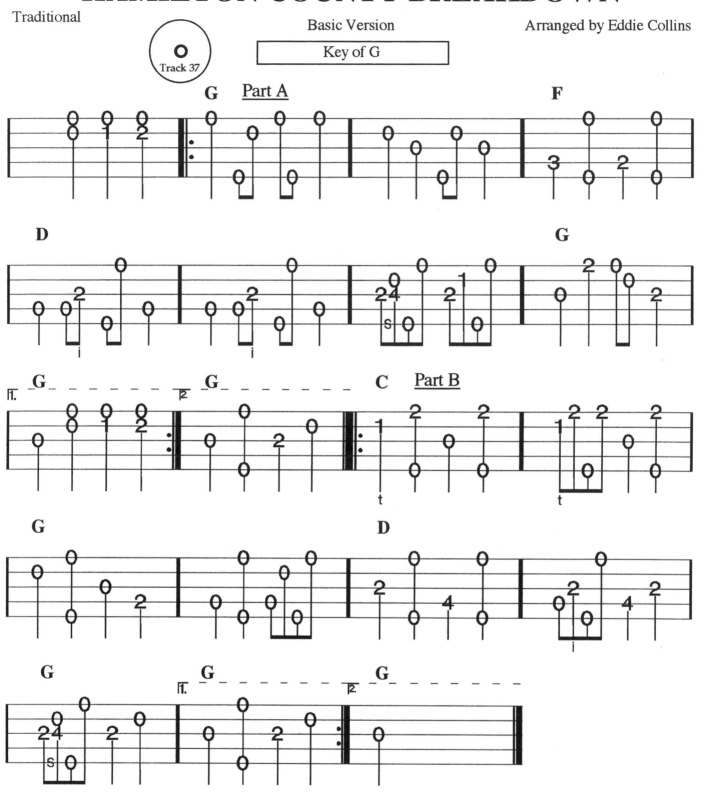

Listen to the recording to understand how to work the Repeats. Begin on beat 2. Use the same number left-hand finger as fret being played, except during the C chord where the 3rd finger plays the 2nd fret on string 1. The 2nd finger also performs the 2 – 4 slide.

HAMILTON COUNTY BREAKDOWN

Traditional   Intermediate Level   Arranged by Eddie Collins

Track 39   Key of G

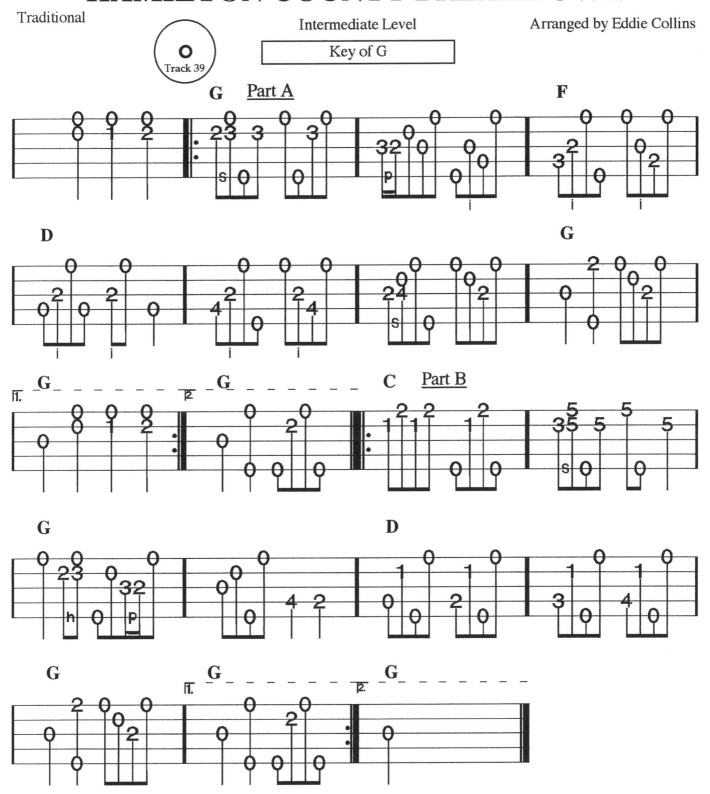

Listen to the recording to understand how to work the Repeats. Begin on beat 2. Slide your 2nd finger from fret 2 to 3 to begin. Then use finger 1 at fret 2 and finger 3 at fret 4 throughout part A. Slide from fret 3 to 5 with the 2nd finger in Part B. Finger 3 then plays fret 5 on string 1. During the D measures, anchor your 1st finger as you add fingers 2, 3 and 4 to frets 2, 3 and 4 on string 4.

HOME SWEET HOME

Traditional

Basic Version

Arranged by Eddie Collins

Track 41

Key of C: Standard G Tuning

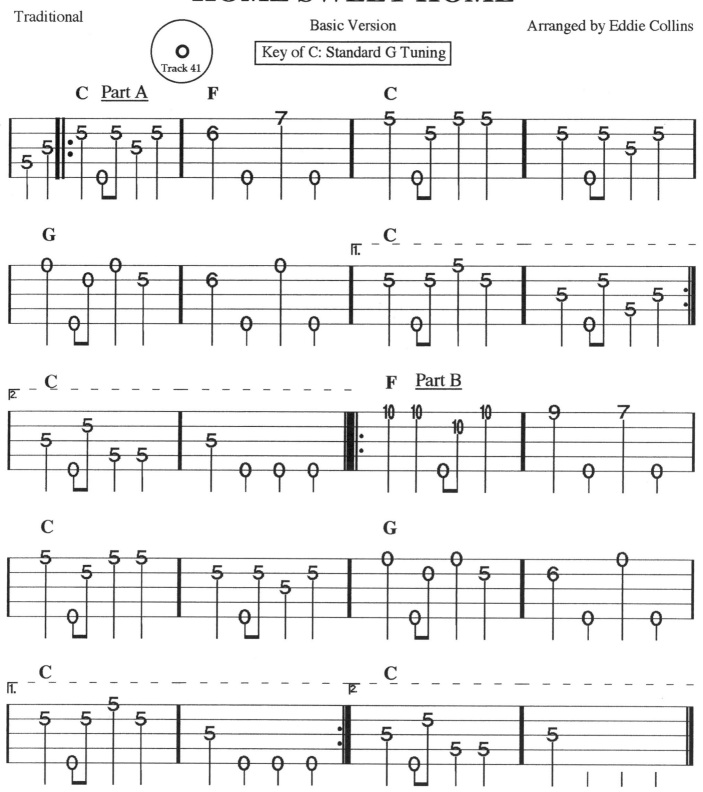

Listen to the recording to understand how to work the Repeats. Begin on beat 3. Play all the 5th fret notes during the C chords as a bar with your 1st finger. Finger 2 plays fret 6 and finger 3 plays fret 7. Use your 1st finger to bar fret 10 to begin Part B. Then move the 1st finger down to frets 9 and 7. Eventually reestablish the bar at fret 5.

28

HOME SWEET HOME

Traditional   Intermediate Level   Arranged by Eddie Collins

Track 43

Key of C: Standard G Tuning

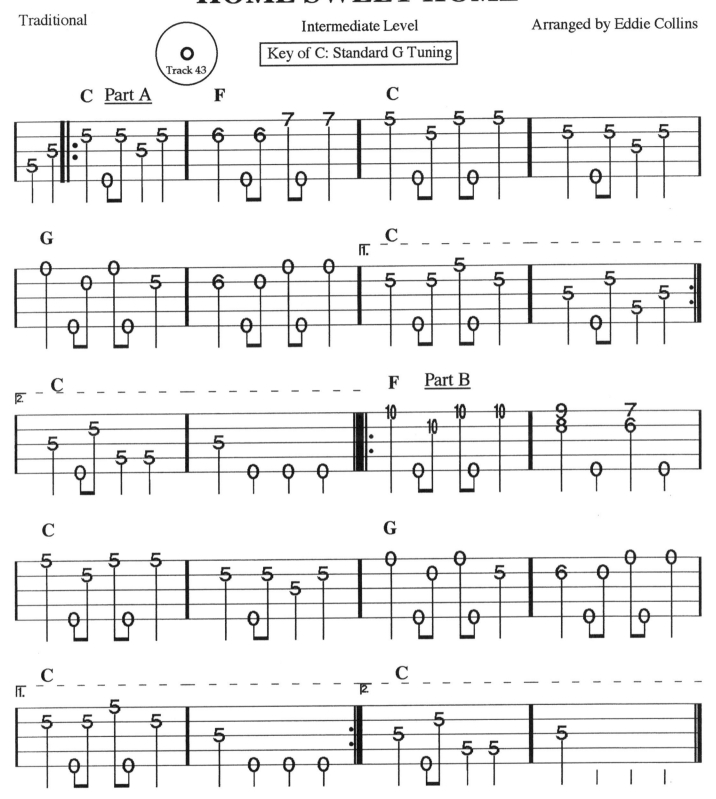

Listen to the recording to understand how the Repeats work. Begin on beat 3 with a bar C chord at the 5th fret. Fingers 2 and 3 then play frets 6 and 7 during the F chord. Use your 1st finger to bar fret 10 to begin Part B. Finger 1 then plays fret 8 while finger 3 plays fret 9. Move this formation down two frets to frets 6 and 7 before returning to your 1st finger bar at fret 5.

LIBERTY

Traditional

Basic Version

Key of D: Standard G Tuning

Track 45

Arranged by Eddie Collins

This solo is in the key of D, but without having to retune the banjo or use a capo. Begin by holding your 1st finger as a bar at the 7th fret. Use your 1st finger to play fret 5 and 2nd finger to play fret 6 during the A chord near the end of Part A. Return to barring the 7th fret on the second beat of the First Ending. Stems with no fret number equal a one-beat rest. The 1st finger plays fret 2 and the 3rd finger plays fret 4 during Part B.

LIBERTY

Traditional

Intermediate Level

Arranged by Eddie Collins

Key of D: Standard G Tuning

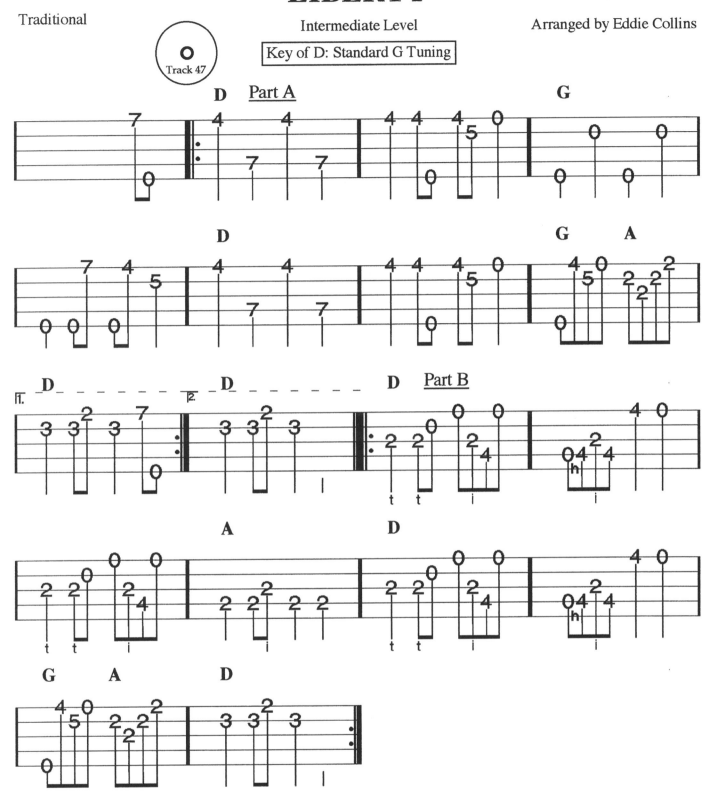

This solo is in the key of D with no retuning or capo. Begin with finger 4 playing the 7th fret and finger 1 playing the 4th fret. Try to hold your 1st finger close to fret 4 as you reach for fret 7 on string 4. Finger 2 plays fret 5. Add finger 2 at fret 3 while holding the bar A chord during the endings. Anchor your 1st finger at fret 2 of string 3 to begin Part B. The 4th finger plays the 4th fret on string 1, except during the next to last measure where the 4th finger plays it. The hammer-ons in Part B are full 8th notes, so don't rush them.

OLD JOE CLARK

Traditional

Basic Version

Arranged by Eddie Collins

Track 49

Key of A: Capo 2nd Fret

Part A

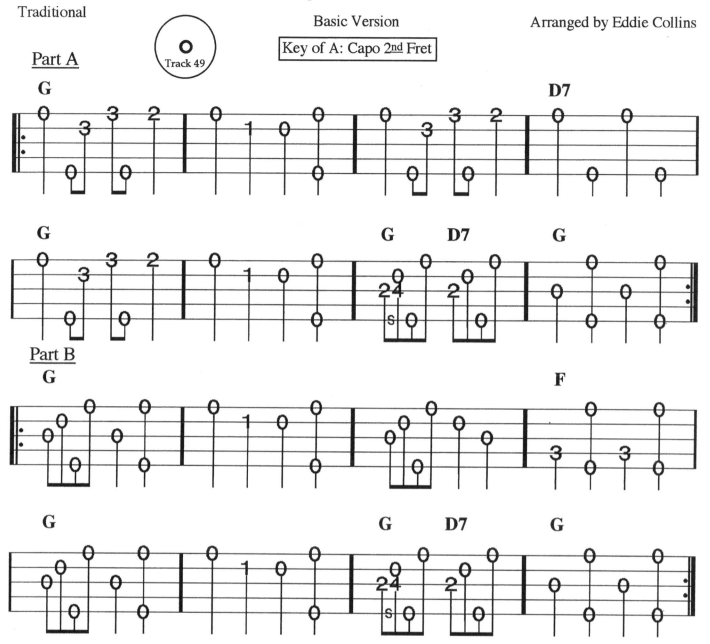

Finger 2 plays fret 3 of string 2 and finger 3 plays fret 3 of string 1. Finger 1 will then play fret 2 on string 1 and move to the 1st fret in the second measure. Perform the 2 – 4 slide with your 2nd finger. You only need to hold the 3rd fret of string 4 during the F chord in Part B.

OLD JOE CLARK

Traditional

Intermediate Level

Arranged by Eddie Collins

Key of A: Capo 2nd Fret

Part A

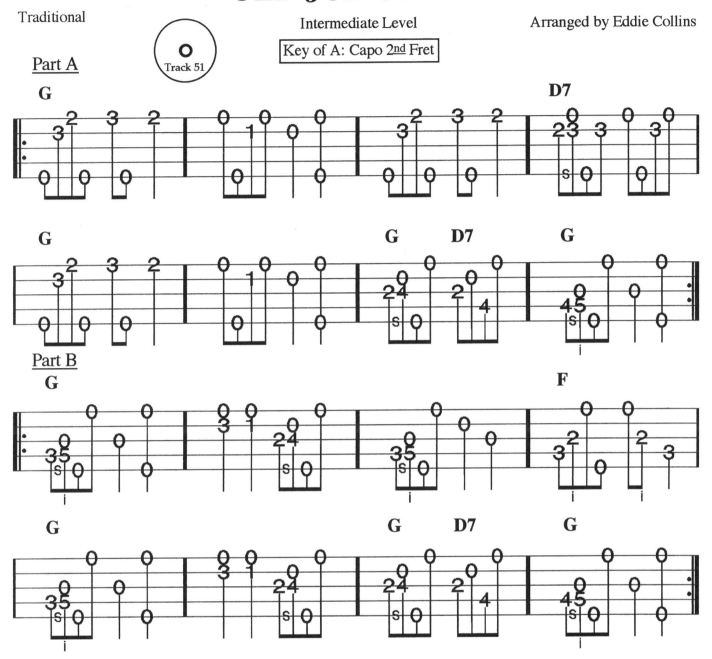

Hold finger 2 on fret 3 of string 2 and finger 1 on fret 2 of string 1 to begin. Finger 3 then plays fret 3 of string 1. Finger 1 will move to the 1st fret in the second measure. Perform the 2 – 4 and 2 – 3 slides with your 2nd finger. Both the 4 – 5 and 3 – 5 slides are performed by your 3rd finger. You only need to hold the 2nd fret on string 3 and the 3rd fret of string 4 during the F chord in Part B. The Index finger plays the open 3rd string on numerous occasions after completing a slide.

RED HAIRED BOY

Traditional

Basic Version

Arranged by Eddie Collins

Key of A: Capo 2nd Fret

Part A

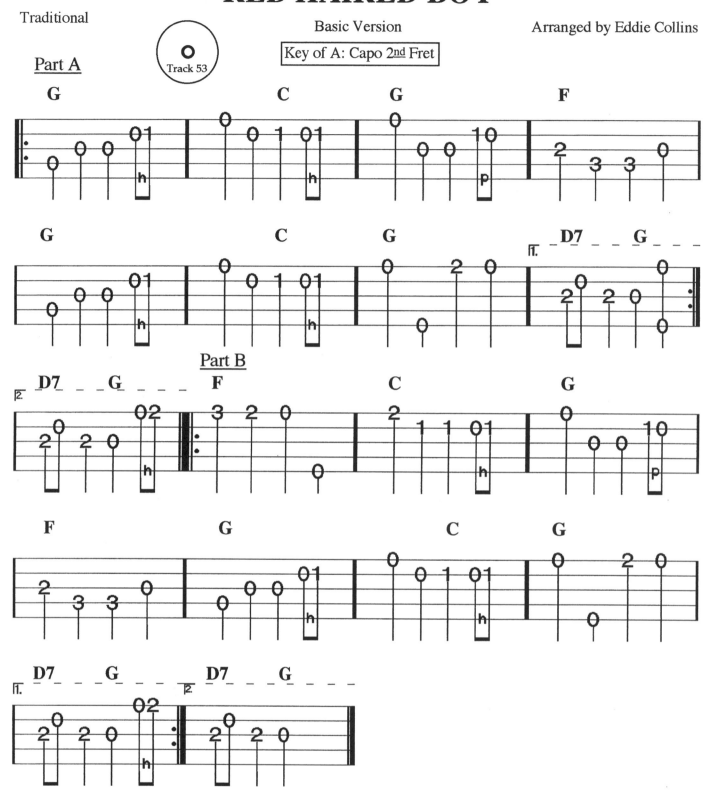

Part B

Use the same number finger as fret being played throughout this piece. Therefore, the 1st finger plays all the hammer-ons and pull-offs except for the hammer-on to the 2nd fret on string 1 during the second ending of Part A leading into Part B. There are no chords to hold, or rolls to play in this arrangement.

RED HAIRED BOY

Traditional

Intermediate Level

Arranged by Eddie Collins

Track 55

Key of A: Capo 2nd Fret

Part A

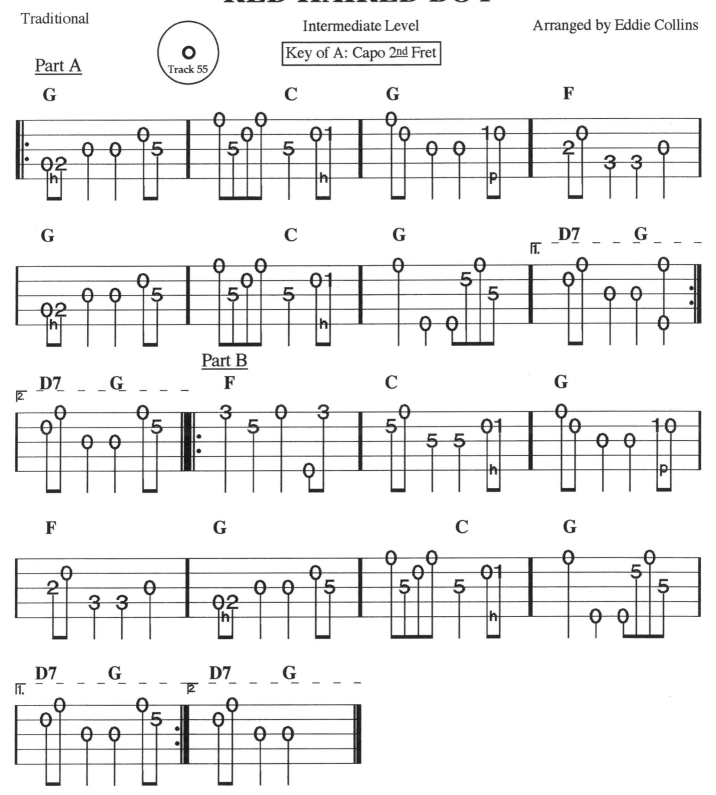

The 3rd finger plays all of the 5th fret notes. You will get a clearer tone if you raise and lower your 3rd finger for each time you play the 5th fret from the end of the first measure through the second measure. Use your 1st finger to play the 3rd fret on string 1 during the first measure of Part B followed by the 3rd finger on the 5th fret. In the second measure. the 2nd finger will play fret 5 on string 3.

35

RED WING

Traditional

Basic Version

Arranged by Eddie Collins

Key of G

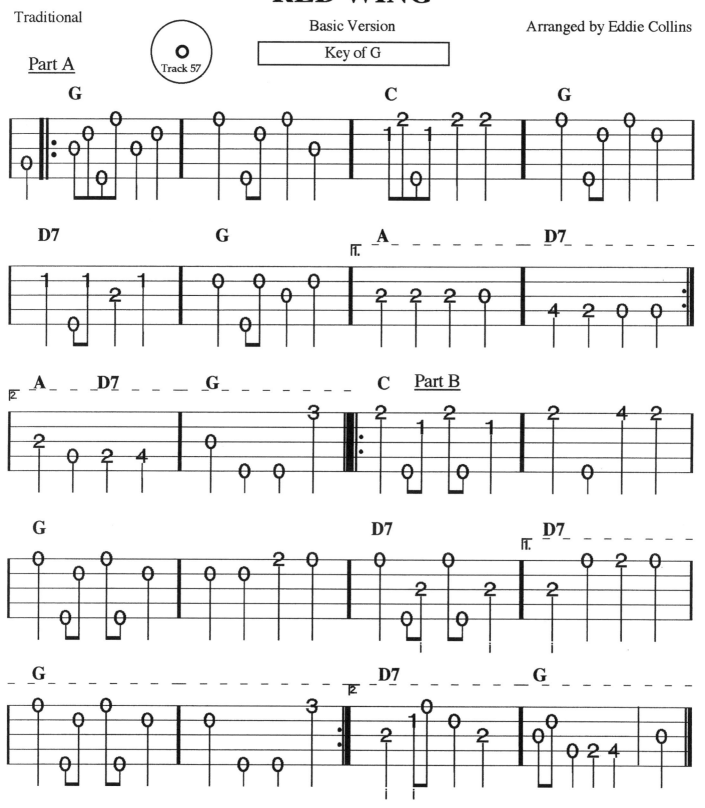

Listen to the recording to understand how to work the Repeats. Begin on beat 4. Use the same number finger as fret being played throughout the piece, except during the C chord where you will use standard C chord fingering. In the second measure of Part B, move the 3rd finger up string 1 to fret 4 and then back to the 2nd fret.

RED WING

Traditional   Intermediate Level   Arranged by Eddie Collins

Key of G

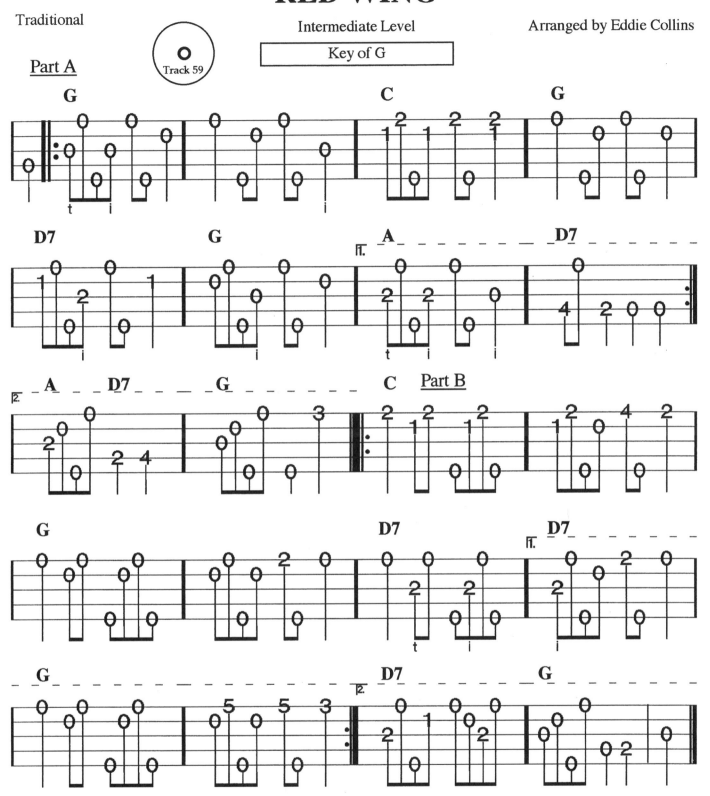

The recording will help you understand how to work the Repeats. Begin on beat 4. The same number finger as fret is played throughout the piece, except during C chords where you use standard C chord fingering. In the second measure of Part B, move the 3rd finger up string 1 to fret 4 and then back to the 2nd fret. The 3rd finger also plays fret 3 on string 1 during the first ending of Part B. Note the many times the Index finger plays string 3 during rolls.

SALT CREEK

Basic Version

Arranged by Eddie Collins

Key of A: Capo 2nd Fret

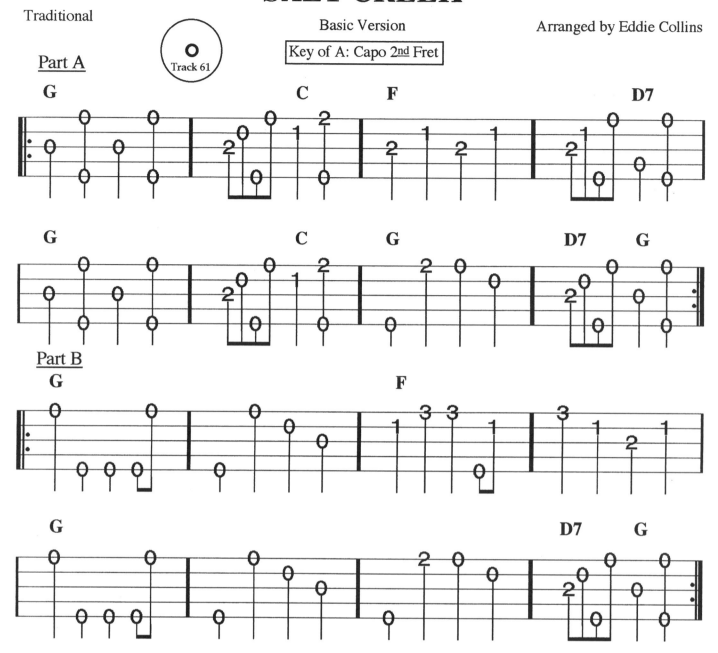

In this version, you can get away with only using fingers 1 and 2 during the F chord in Part A. It will feel as though you are playing a D7. Hold finger 1 on fret 1 and finger 4 on fret 3 during the F chord in Part B. You can let go of the 4th finger after playing the first note in the fourth measure of Part B.

SALT CREEK

Traditional   Intermediate Level   Arranged by Eddie Collins

Track 63

Key of A: Capo 2nd Fret

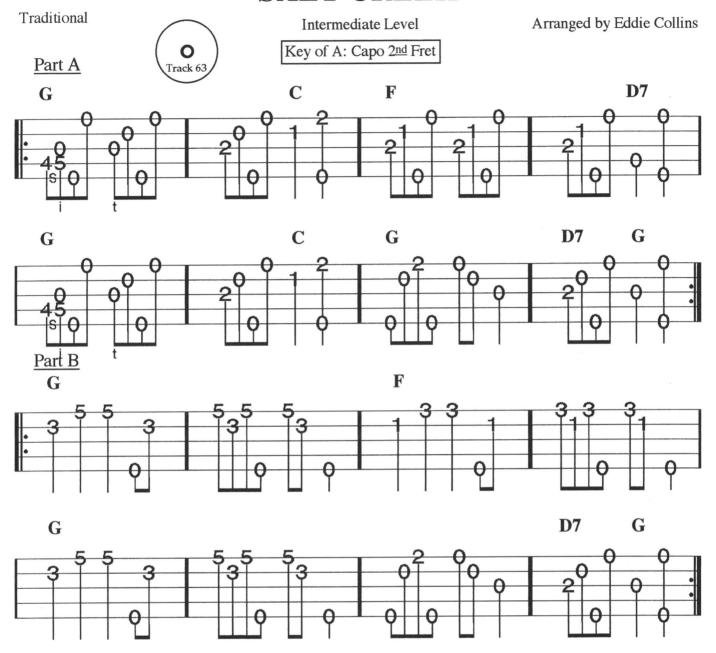

The right-hand Index finger strikes string 3 right as you complete the 4–5 slide with the left hand during measures 1 and 5. It will feel as though you are playing a D7 during the F chord in Part A. Hold finger 1 on fret 3 and finger 4 on fret 5 during the G chord to begin Part B. Move fingers 1 and 4 down to frets 1 and 3 respectively during the F chord in Part B.

SOLDIER'S JOY

Traditional

Basic Version

Arranged by Eddie Collins

Track 65

Key of D: Standard G Tuning

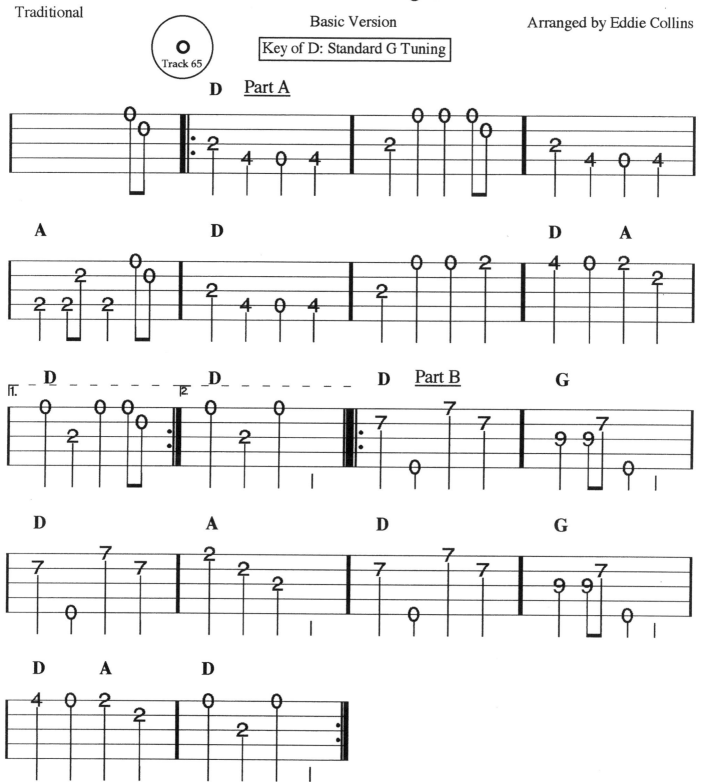

This solo is in the key of D without retuning the banjo. The 1st finger plays fret 2 and the 3rd finger plays fret 4 during Part A. Bar your 1st finger for the A chord. Bar fret 7 to begin Part B. Finger 3 will then play the 9th fret. Stems with no fret number equal a one-beat rest.

SOLDIER'S JOY

Traditional

Intermediate Level

Arranged by Eddie Collins

Key of D: Standard G Tuning

Track 67

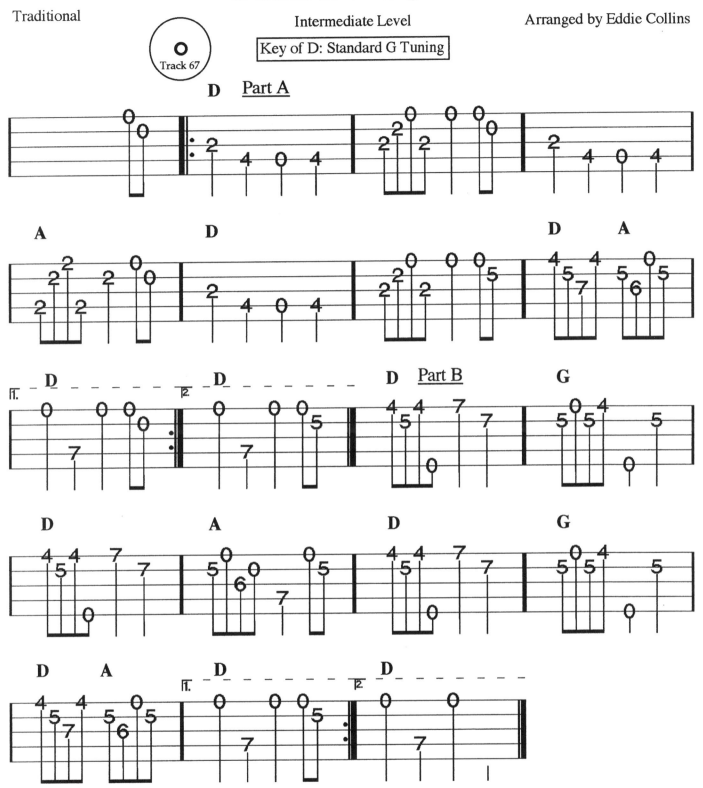

This solo is in the key of D without retuning the banjo. The 1st finger plays fret 2 on string 3 and the 3rd finger plays fret 4 on string 4 during Part A. The 2nd finger plays fret 2 on string 2. Starting with the next to last measure of Part A, line up fingers 1 – 4 at frets 4 – 7. Also use this fingering throughout Part B, including barring strings 1 and 2 at fret 7 with the 4th finger.

WHISKEY BEFORE BREAKFAST

Traditional

Basic Version

Arranged by Eddie Collins

Track 69

Key of D; 5th String A: a DGBD

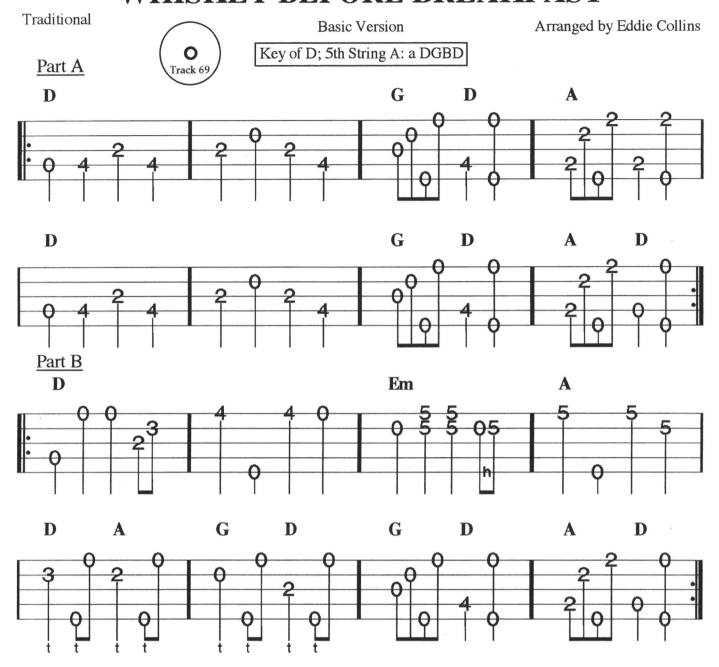

Tune the 5th string up to the note A while keeping all the other strings in standard G tuning. Anchor your 1st finger on fret 2 of string 3 to begin. Your 3rd finger will play the 4th fret notes. Finger 3 plays the 5th fret on string 1 during the Em chord in Part B. Add your 2nd finger to string 2, fret 5 and use it for the hammer-on at the end of the measure. Move your 2nd finger down to fret 3 to begin the descending run in the last line. Note the use of the Thumb on the 2nd string during the final line.

WHISKEY BEFORE BREAKFAST

Traditional   Intermediate Level   Arranged by Eddie Collins

Track 71

Key of D; 5th String A: a DGBD

Part A

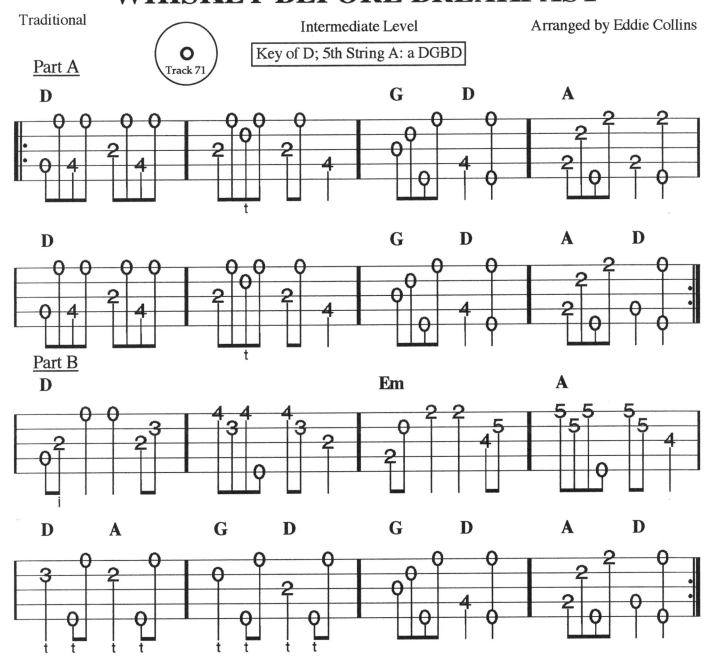

Part B

Tune the 5th string up to the note A. Anchor your 1st finger on fret 2 of string 3 to begin Parts A and B. The open 1st string notes serve as a drone, instead of the 5th string. Your 3rd finger will play the 4th fret notes during Part A.

Hold a D chord beginning with the last beat of the first measure of Part B. Finger 1 will hold the 4th fret of string 3 during the Em chord, followed by finger 2 on fret 5 of string 2 on the following note and finger 3 on fret 5 of string 1 in the A chord measure. Move your 2nd finger down to fret 3 to begin the descending run in the last line. Note the use of the Thumb on the 2nd string during the final line.

More Great Banjo Books from Centerstream...